Original title:
The Current's Embrace

Copyright © 2025 Creative Arts Management OÜ
All rights reserved.

Author: Jaxon Kingsley
ISBN HARDBACK: 978-1-80587-461-4
ISBN PAPERBACK: 978-1-80587-931-2

A Stream of Consciousness

In the river of thought, where ideas swim,
I met a fish wearing a top hat, so prim.
He winked and said, 'Life's just a jest!'
'I skipped breakfast; now I'm a mess!'

Bubbles burst with giggles, oh what a sound,
A turtle in sneakers is racing around.
He shouted, 'Catch me, if you can, you slowpoke!'
I tripped on a log, what a funny joke!

The water flows by with a splash and a swirl,
A frog croaked a tune, gave his throat a twirl.
I joined in the chorus, off-key and loud,
Our symphony attracted a curious crowd!

As sunlight danced down, casting shadows so bright,
A squirrel disguised as a mermaid took flight.
'I'm just here for the nuts!' he declared with a grin,
In this stream of odd thoughts, where fun's sure to win!

In the Wake of Shared Desires

Floating on laughter's wave,
We chase our dreams like fish with braves.
Banana peels and rubber ducks,
We dance through puddles, oh, what luck!

With every splash, a giggle burst,
In these silly moments, we quench our thirst.
Like jellybeans tossed in a stream,
Together we paddle, chasing the dream!

A Journey Through the Swelling Waters

Bobbing about on a flimsy raft,
Canoeing our way to the land of craft.
With each twist and turn, we try to steer,
Riding the waves while sipping on beer.

Oh, what a ride, let's hold on tight,
For waves don't care if we tumble or fight.
Sipping our coffee as we make our way,
Coffee spills over—what a clumsy display!

Currents of Solace and Serenity

In this bubbling brook of pure delight,
We leap like frogs, what a silly sight.
Each splash a reminder, we don't take care,
As laughter erupts, we forget our despair.

With dogs chasing sticks and cats purring near,
We've found our quiet, we've conquered our fear.
In the flow of chuckles, there's warmth all around,
In the whirlpool of fun, we've truly found ground!

The Rhythm of Shifting Waters

The tide dances like a goofy friend,
Pulling us in, around every bend.
Skipping our worries, we twirl and spin,
Riding the waves, let the laughter begin!

We wear rubber boots; they squeak with glee,
As we leap through puddles, wild and free.
With playful jests, we splash and jive,
In this wacky world, we feel so alive!

Unseen Currents

Beneath the surface, fish do laugh,
As bubbles rise, they take a bath.
In tangled weeds, they play all day,
While sea cucumbers hide away.

Jellyfish dance, all floaty and free,
"Is this a party?" asks Mr. Glee.
Starfish cheer as they spin around,
Clapping their arms with no sound found.

Embracing the Flow

Silly ducks glide, quacking in rhyme,
Trying to waddle, but slipping in time.
They flap and they flop, making quite the scene,
With feathered friends, they're the laughing machine.

The river chuckles, rocks chuckle too,
As turtles glide by, feeling brand new.
"Why walk when you've got this nice stream?"
Says a wise old otter, living the dream.

Serene Reflections

Mirror, mirror, on the lake,
Who's the silliest, make no mistake?
Frogs leap high, with splashes and flair,
While dragonflies dodge, buzzing the air.

Ripples giggle, dancing on light,
As beavers wear hats, oh what a sight!
With sticks as their props, they're putting on plays,
In the watery world where fun always stays.

Waters of Connection

Lilypads float, like boats in a line,
While fish swap gossip, and share some wine.
Crabs crack jokes, all in good fun,
Under the sun, until day is done.

Waterbugs prance, like dancers on stage,
In their aquatic ballet, they engage.
"Join us, dear friend!" the currents call,
In this whimsical world, where laughter's the ball.

Fluid Harmonies

In streams where fish wear hats, they chat,
Flowing past the trees where squirrels dance and pat.
Bubbles rise, a flurry of giggling delight,
As crabs in tuxedos don't mind the night.

Rafts made of marshmallows drift away,
With jellybeans bobbing, leading the fray.
A playful splash, a prankster's laugh escapes,
In this liquid symphony, joy reshapes.

Essence of the Undercurrents

Beneath the surface, fish hold a ball,
Sardines dressed in stripes, they are having a ball.
Seahorses wear glasses, debating the sport,
Making waves over who brings the best report.

Octopuses juggle, their arms in a spin,
While pufferfish chuckle, striking a grin.
Pearls of wisdom float on by with a tease,
In a world where joy flows with fresh, briny breeze.

In the Wake of Warm Currents

Sunbeams dance like frogs on a lake,
With turtles surfing, oh what a break!
Dolphins wear shades, enjoying the ride,
While clams doze off in their sandy tide.

Water lilies gossip, share secrets and schemes,
Creating ripples that burst into dreams.
A party of plankton, having a blast,
In the warmth of the wave, good times are cast.

Fluidity and Freedom

Streams of laughter swirl like a song,
Where jellyfish twirl, feeling so strong.
Frogs in flip-flops celebrate with cheer,
As they leap and glide with no trace of fear.

Fish throw a fiesta, turning in styles,
With bubbles as balloons, they dance in miles.
Underwater, the fun never takes a break,
With every twist and turn, new joys they make.

Embraced by the Waters

A fish swam by with a grin so wide,
I asked for tips on the surfing tide.
He said, "Just flop! You'll find your way,"
And off he flipped, in a splashy play.

With my floatie duck, I took the dive,
Giggling hard, I felt so alive.
The waves danced back with a cheeky cheer,
As I paddled around, forgetting my fear.

A River's Soliloquy

The river spoke with a bubbling sound,
Telling jokes to the rocks all around.
"Why did the fish refuse to play?"
"He thought it might rain on his parade!"

I chuckled as I drifted along,
The breeze hummed gently a silly song.
Each ripple laughed, each splash was a shout,
As the sun joined in, waving about.

Touching the Depths

Diving down where the seaweed grows,
I found an octopus wearing old clothes.
He winked at me with a mischievous eye,
"You can't catch me; I'm too sly!"

I chased him around with bubbles in tow,
Swapping tales of the undertow.
He finally paused, gave me a grin,
"Who knew swimming could be such a win?"

Echoes of Tranquil Waters

The pond reflected a frog in a hat,
Singing a tune that was quite chitchat.
"Why croak alone when you can serenade?"
He leaped with flair, in a splash parade!

The dragonflies giggled, their wings quite bright,
Joining the fun in the soft evening light.
As the moon peeked out, with a wink and a beam,
I laughed at the joys of this watery dream.

Embracing the Current

In the river where ducks parade,
One tried a dive, but instead it brayed.
A fish laughed hard, wobbling away,
As bubbles rose to join the play.

The rocks got jealous, looking so dry,
They splashed around, giving it a try.
But slippery grins couldn't be outdone,
As a turtle slid past, basking in fun.

Streams of Identity

A fish told tales of swimming fast,
While a turtle claimed to be the cast.
In cast-off hats, they formed a crew,
Belly flops were a common view.

The currents whispered secrets bold,
Of mermaid parties, treasures of gold.
But when the octopus joined the fun,
He inked the scene—how they did run!

The Fluidity of Being

Bubbles giggled, floating high,
While crabs engaged in a dance nearby.
They shuffled sideways, what a sight!
Called it the funky underwater bite.

In this giggle stream, all things collide,
Where even a rock has a wiggly side.
But when the waves thump, who can keep still?
The seaweed twirls, always ready to thrill.

Harmony in Motion

The waves were jamming, oh what a beat,
As fish threw parties with jellyfish sweet.
They bounced and swayed, quite out of line,
While sea cucumbers passed on the wine.

A dolphin sang a funny old tune,
While starfish laughed, changing the moon.
In this watery world, all joined the dance,
For every splash ignites a chance!

Buoyed by Trust and Tenderness

A rubber duck floats with great pride,
While dolphins dance right by its side.
A curious fish gives a little wink,
They toss around ideas, and then they think.

The sunbeams giggle on the surface bright,
As a turtle giggles, taking flight.
The bubbles say secrets, all gooey and sweet,
In this silly world, even fish have feet.

Streams of Reflection and Growth

A mirror of water, so shiny and clear,
Where frogs tell jokes, and crickets cheer.
They mirror the clouds that tumble and sway,
Making reflections of the most hilarious play.

In the depth of the stream, with splashes around,
The catfish tell tales of the friends they've found.
With laughter as ripples, they tickle the flow,
Growing giggles and gags, as the waters bestow.

Merging Paths Along the Riverbank

Two paths come together with a playful twist,
Where otters connect, making plans not to miss.
They hold onto life with a wink and a shout,
Finding joy in the merge, that's what it's about.

Alongside the banks, they trip and they slip,
Oh, watch as they gawk with a chuckle and quip!
Embracing each puddle, they leap with delight,
As the river observes, chuckling in the night.

The Sway of Ebb and Flow

The tides like dancers in a silly ballet,
With waves that giggle and twist and sway.
Crabs gather round, snapping claws in a game,
While seagulls cackle, and they take aim.

Each rise brings a chuckle, each fall a joke,
As the shore tells a story, making folks poke.
In the rhythm of water, a joy that we know,
The laughter of nature, in ebb and in flow.

Waves of Heartfelt Connection

In the pool, I tried to dive,
Belly flop, I barely survived.
The laughter bubbles, floats above,
Splashing joy, that's what I love.

Water fights and silly games,
Ducking under, calling names.
A wave of giggles hits the sand,
With every splash, we join a band.

Rubber ducks and sun-kissed skin,
Race the ripples, let's begin!
Floating on, we lose our cares,
Together, dancing with our flares.

Friends unite, we'd never lose,
In this sea of silly shoes.
Riding tides of joy and cheer,
Water's laughter, loud and clear.

Underneath the Surface

Beneath the waves, fish wear a grin,
Do they know how fun it's been?
Shrimp in shades, doing ballet,
Crabs in caps, what a display!

An octopus with eight left feet,
Dancing clumsily, quite the treat.
Seaweed sways like a hairdo bold,
Fishtails flick like stories told.

Bubbles pop like tiny jokes,
Jellyfish in neon cloaks.
Flip-flop laughter, oh what a sight,
Underneath, it's pure delight!

Join the fiesta with a splash,
As starfish do the underwater bash.
Giggles ripple through the sea,
Even the waves are laughing free!

The Life Beneath

Coral crabs with tiny hats,
Sipping tea with fancy sprats.
Seahorses prance in posh attire,
Twisting round like they retire.

Bubble-blowing pirates tease,
Playing tag with effortless ease.
A clam clinks cups for a toast,
To the fish who dance the most!

Oysters wink, what a sly bunch,
Shucking jokes for a lunchtime crunch.
Laughter flows like the tide's embrace,
In the hustle and bustle, we find our place.

With every splash, the fun grows vast,
Where treasures hide, we've come to cast.
Beneath the waves, life's a play,
In this underworld, we laugh all day!

Symphony of Streams

Drifting along, it's quite a ride,
Bumpy waters, let's glide and slide.
A frog on a log sings off-key,
While turtles giggle in harmony.

Ripples laugh, and the wind chimes in,
As fish orchestrate a finny din.
With a plop and a splash, the show begins,
Nature's concert, where fun always wins!

Raindrops join like a full band,
Tapping rhythms on soft sand.
Each melody swirls with glee,
In this stream, we're wild and free.

So come along, let's make a cheer,
With splashes and laughs, our hearts are near.
In the water's symphony, we sway and spin,
Together forever, with a joyful grin!

The Confluence of Dreams

In a river where dreams collide,
A fish wore a hat and said with pride.
Turtles recite in poetic tones,
While otters form bands with bubble phones.

Splashed laughter dances on the waves,
Where mermaids complain of the sun's hot braves.
A boat floats by, with cats that sing,
Promising joy in every swing.

In this festival of whimsy and cheer,
We dodge the bubbles, sip on our beer.
Dreams and fish swim in synchronized dives,
As the flavors of fun keep us alive!

Embracing the Drift

A leaf on the water, it twirled and twirled,
As frogs sang sweet songs, their harmony swirled.
The wind took a nap, oh so sublime,
While fish formed a conga line just in time.

Crabs painted nails with the finest sheen,
Debating the best color for the marine.
With laughter erupting and glee on display,
Nature's own circus, come join the fray!

A snail on a surfboard, can you believe?
With shells full of dreams that he promises to weave.
We're all in this dance, let's not be stiff,
Embrace the odd, it's the ultimate gift!

Liquid Journeys

Watermelon boats float by in the sun,
With squishy sweet laughter, oh what fun!
Dancing ducks in a synchronized line,
While jellybeans bubble in the sweet brine.

A crab juggles seashells, quite the trick,
While sea urchins giggle at his slick flick.
In this fluid world where silliness reigns,
Every drop sings joy through laughter's refrains!

We ride on the waves of the silliest dreams,
With fish that wear glasses and talk in teams.
A boat full of laughter, our spirits ablaze,
In the joy of the water, we'll happily bask.

Beneath the Surface of Silence

Bubbles are whispers in the water's sway,
As a crab tries to riddle and fails in dismay.
A clam plays the banjo, quite out of tune,
While dolphins throw parties beneath the moon.

Octopuses juggle with skill and flair,
While snails sport mustaches, a fabulous affair.
With laughter echoing through waters so deep,
It's the silliest secret that we all keep!

In a world where whispers become joyful shouts,
We dive into fun, forgetting our doubts.
Let's swim in the laughter, let's splash in delight,
For beneath the silence, life dances bright!

Harmonies in the Rippling Abyss

In a sea of giggles and grins,
Sardines tap dance, where silliness wins.
Jellyfish sway to a jelly-like beat,
While starfish enjoy their sand-soaked seat.

Dolphins leap, wearing sunglasses too,
While crabs play poker on a bright blue cue.
Mermaids sing off-key, with flair and fun,
As waves form laughter, shining like the sun.

Embraced by the Liquid Horizon

Waves waddle in, a curious parade,
Surfboards slip and slide, charades in spade.
Octopuses juggle, while seals play chess,
With a splash of folly, there's never a mess.

Nemo found his friends at a fancy ball,
Fish in tuxedos doing the backstraw crawl.
With seaweed confetti raining from above,
A bubbly soirée, everyone falls in love.

Navigating the Undercurrents of Love

A lighthouse flickers, with a wink and a grin,
While boats flirt shyly, their engines spin.
Crabs hold hands in a clumsy embrace,
As love drifts by at a comical pace.

Seahorses dance in a watery swirl,
Chasing each other, as soft currents twirl.
The jelly drips laughter, like candy from sea,
In this fishy affair, love's free as a spree.

Rafting on Streams of Memory

Floating on laughter, we drift and we glide,
With a quack from a duck and a wise turtle's ride.
Wet socks are a treasure, unclaimed and worn,
As memories bubble from rivers reborn.

Paddles break the silence, with splashes galore,
Canoes are giggling, wanting to explore.
When the marshmallow peeps skitter and sway,
We raft through the memories, come out to play.

Ebbing Dreams

Floating in scrappy boats,
Chasing after sleepy goats.
Waves tickle toes with glee,
While fish throw parties, oh what a spree!

Banana peels surfing by,
Alligators in bow ties.
Silly hats upon my head,
As I sail a marshmallow bed.

With jellybean sails, we drift,
Complaining 'bout our absent gift.
Coconuts laugh from the shore,
Their giggles make the mermaids snore.

Pirates juggling jellyfish,
Chasing some elusive wish.
In this wild water so bright,
Even ducks can dance all night!

Undercurrents of Serenity

Underneath the twinkling waves,
Clams recite their happy raves.
Seaweed dances with delight,
While crabs start a conga night.

Turtles spinning in retreat,
Pretending they're on swanky feet.
With bubbles forming silly charts,
They're making art with ocean hearts.

A playful otter flips and spins,
As he challenges the ocean fins.
Sea cucumbers get high with glee,
Claiming they're the swag of the sea.

Seagulls sport their trendy shades,
While dolphins play in grand parades.
In this tranquil, cheeky flow,
Even the tides just want to glow!

Caresses of the River

The river winks with little splashes,
As turtles wear their sassy mustaches.
Bubbles pop like tiny cheers,
While the fish share silly fears.

Canoes drift in playful chase,
As frogs hop in a froggy race.
With dragonflies selling bling,
Everyone's happy, wanting to sing.

Leaves gossip upon the tide,
As beavers try to take a ride.
The whispers of cool, fresh air,
Tickle noses without a care.

Merry ducks prance in a line,
Only to slip on rocks, divine.
With laughter echoing in their wake,
The river's got the best heartache!

Liquid Grace

In a world of flowing giggles,
Water striders break into wiggles.
Splashing joy with each quick dart,
While fish hold hands, forming art.

Daisies float on fluffy dreams,
In this land of silly schemes.
With butterflies wearing bright ties,
They're having fun under wide skies.

Bubbles race like little trains,
Chasing sunlight over lanes.
Waves bounce in a playful chase,
Each ripple's a chuckle, a warm embrace.

As raindrops decide to dance,
Puddles giggle at their chance.
Liquid grace flows through the air,
Spreading laughter everywhere!

Serene Surges of Unspoken Words

In the river of chatty fish,
They tell tales with a swish.
A bubble of laughter goes by,
And splashes of giggles fill the sky.

Blabbering minnows swim to and fro,
Sharing secrets only they know.
An octopus jokes, with a twist of ink,
While turtles ponder and start to think.

Fishes whisper, 'Did you hear that?'
While a wise old catfish chatters like a brat.
Oh, the stories beneath the waves,
Of playful pranks and silly knaves.

The current flows with a wink and a grin,
As seaweed dances where laughter begins.
With all this fun underneath the sun,
Who knew fish could get so much done?

The Flow of Moments Shared

Bouncing bubbles greet the day,
Who knew fun was just a sway?
A shrimp does the cha-cha with glee,
While a crab's doing the crabby-key.

Sardines pack a punchline each time,
Their jokes are worse, but still rhyme.
Mussels chuckle at passing boats,
'Look at those land fins—beat their coats!'

The tides roll in with gaffaw and chime,
Gulls join in, they sway to the rhyme.
What a splash of joy in the stream,
Moments flow like a silly dream!

Prawns pull a prank, making waves feign,
They turn the tide to laughter's refrain.
Underwater shenanigans never cease,
In this splashy realm where spirits release.

Tracing the Currents of Tomorrow

With flippers flailing, the otters glide,
Sharing jokes as they slip and slide.
'Why don't fish play piano?' they jest,
'Because they can't tuna!'—laughter's the best!

In schools where guppies share their tales,
Witty repartee is the wind in their sails.
The playful waves toss around ideas,
As seabass giggle without any fears.

Mermaids chuckle while brushing their hair,
'What's a fish's favorite instrument? A squale!'
As laughter bubbles through sandy nooks,
Tomorrow holds joy, so let's write the books!

From shaft to gulf, with a wink and a wave,
We dive into fun, be bold, be brave.
Tracing these currents in torrents of play,
Let smiles ripple and brighten the day!

Flowing Whispers

The brook babbles secrets so sly,
While frogs croak jokes as they hop by.
'Why did the fish blush?' they shout,
'It saw the ocean's bottom and ran out!'

With splashes of joy curling in the air,
The turtles chimed, 'Great, we're all bare!'
Around the bend, otters frolic and spin,
Organizing parties where all can join in.

Murmurs of laughter drift like a breeze,
As fishes tease, 'Don't swim with the trees!'
Shimmers of giggles paint the surface light,
With every ripple, the world feels just right.

In this flowing tapestry, spirits unite,
Where whimsy and joy set the scene so bright.
So gather your tales, let them drift and play,
For laughter's the treasure that never decays!

Water's Tender Song

Splashing about with glee,
Fish join in, chuckling free.
A duck takes a silly dive,
All the waves seem to connive.

Rain falls down, a friendly tease,
Puddles form, dance with the breeze.
Umbrellas bob like jellybeans,
Nature's jokes, full of routines.

Sunlight sparkles, a winking eye,
Clouds float by, on laughter fly.
A frog croaks out a punchline phrase,
Water sings in silly ways.

Bubbles rise with a gentle pop,
Hilarity won't ever stop.
With every splash a new delight,
The stream plays on, day and night.

Interlaced Reflections

Mirrors dance upon the shore,
Waves giggle, wanting more.
A fish gives a quirky grin,
Reflections twist and spin.

Ripples play with shimmering light,
Making shadows leap from sight.
A flamingo prances about,
Dancing proudly, no doubt.

The sun joins in, a warm ray,
Tricking clouds to join the play.
Nature's jest in vibrant hue,
Laughter shared by me and you.

Beneath the surface, tales unfold,
Of fishy puns and laughs untold.
Each splish-splash a fresh new jest,
In the water's playful quest.

In the Wake of Change

The tide rolls in with a cheeky grin,
Even crabs won't shy from a spin.
Seashells gather to share their views,
Chatting loudly in various hues.

The wind teases the waves to rise,
Whispers of laughter in disguise.
Seagulls caw with a mocking jest,
In their eyes, a treasure chest.

Storm clouds gather, but who's afraid?
Lightning strikes with a joke well laid.
Thunder rumbling can't help but guffaw,
As splashes paint the earth's grand law.

When the calm returns, oh what a sight!
The sea glimmers, tossing pure delight.
In every wave, there lies a chance,
To find the fun in nature's dance.

Dance of Elements

Water twirls with flame's bright cheer,
Creating laughter's sweet frontier.
Earth joins in, steady and wise,
While air tickles the playful skies.

Springs of joy bubble and whirl,
While breezes around them gently twirl.
Each element hums a tune,
Chasing clouds beneath the moon.

Even rocks can't help but chuckle,
As waves tickle, soft and subtle.
The sun pops in, with a radiant wink,
Turning thoughts to laughter's link.

In this ballet of joy and jest,
Nature performs her silly quest.
With every swirl and gleeful spin,
Life's a dance we all can win.

Tides of Tranquility

In a sea of socks, lost and found,
My woes float by without a sound.
The waves tickle toes, oh what a jest,
A swim in chaos, I'm quite a mess.

My boat made of cork, it bobs with glee,
Chased by a fish who's teasing me.
He splashed and laughed, such a sly wink,
Dare I dive in, or just stay and sink?

With seagulls circling, plotting my fate,
They steal my fries; they can't wait.
Yet laughter is squished like sand in a shoe,
The tides pull me in, but I'm stuck like glue.

So here's to the splash, the giggle and cheer,
Life's wobbly boat always brings good beer.
With each tiny wave, a grinning embrace,
I float through the tides, a scrambling face.

Embrace of the Stream

Along the stream, I found a seat,
Sat on a rock, it felt quite neat.
The dragonflies zoomed, a bustling crowd,
Each one shouting, 'We'll take you out loud!'

A turtle peeked, with a wink and blink,
Came over to say, 'Yo, what do you think?'
He brought his buddies, the frogs and newts,
We danced like fools in our muddy boots.

The water splashed as I tried to sway,
But tripped on a root, oh what a display!
The giggling creek stole my proud whisper,
A splash of hilarity, I was a twister.

So here I am, with nature's best band,
Dancing with fish to our own silly brand.
Each ripple a laugh, a story to beam,
A joyous frolic in the bubbling stream.

Dance of Rippling Waves

The ocean's a party, come one, come all,
With dolphins doing the can-can, oh how they sprawl!
Seaweed confetti flutters down with grace,
While crabs show their moves—what a quirky space!

A starfish rolled by, waving a hand,
Shouting out tunes, isn't this grand?
The fish flipped flopped in a synchronized show,
While the clam threw a tantrum, 'Don't steal my flow!'

With every splash, the giggles grew loud,
As jellyfish glided like they were proud.
But oh, there's a lesson in this spunky dance—
Avoid the tug of a seaweed romance!

So let's sway to the rhythm, join in the fun,
Make memories with waves till the day is done.
In the tide's playful hug, let's frolic and roam,
In the dance of the waves, we all find a home.

Windswept Caress

A gust blew through my disheveled hair,
Made me feel like I was some kind of flair.
I strutted along with a floppy hat,
Till the wind wrestled it off—oh, how 'bout that?

It tumbled away, like a runaway car,
Chased by the breeze like a movie star.
The trees laughed hard, waving their limbs,
I scrambled and pounced, oh, on my whims!

With kites in the sky, they giggled and twirled,\nTheir
colorful sails danced, all whirled and swirled.
I couldn't keep up with their gusty grace,
Wind's wild embrace spun me in place!

But still, I laugh with each breezy shove,
For nature's a prankster with all its love.
So here's to the wind, with its cheeky cheer,
In its playful hold, I shed every fear!

The Touch of Water

A splash and a laugh, here we go,
Dripping like ice cream, oh no, oh no!
Feet in the puddle, dancing around,
Why do we always trip on the ground?

Waves of giggles, dashing away,
Trying to catch fish that just want to play.
Sailing on rafts made of old pizza boxes,
Navigating floods with our soggy sockses.

Ducks watch us closely, quacking their cheer,
Wondering what's happening, with such a veneer.
Throwing some bread, look, they're taking a dive,
Who knew at this age, we'd still be alive?

Skimming the surface, our shadows dance,
Silly mistakes, but we never glance.
With water balloons, we start a grand fight,
Our laughter echoes under the moonlight.

Murmurs in Motion

Ripples of laughter in a small stream,
Bounce like rubber balls in a crazy dream.
Oh, catch that frog! But he's quite the sneak,
Jumping away with a cheeky little peak.

Fish swim by, with a giggle or two,
They must think we're silly, oh how we goo!
Splashes and splatters, it's a wild ride,
Floating and drifting, we giggle with pride.

Racing the tide, we're a sight to behold,
In our makeshift boats of cardboard and gold.
Falling off edges, landing with flair,
Hoping that nobody's watching us stare.

The winds join the fun, rustling leaves,
Tickling our noses, as the water weaves.
With buckets and spoons, the best way to play,
Every splash counts, come join our fray!

Where Rivers Meet

When rivers collide, it's a wacky show,
Like two pals arguing with nowhere to go.
Twisting and turning, the water's alive,
Making up stories that surely can thrive.

Boats made of logs float by with a grin,
As turtles do yoga, their tails in a spin.
Catch the weird fish; it's a carnival set,
Flipping and flopping, no time for regret.

Otters are laughing, sliding with ease,
Creating a splash, just avoiding the trees.
Oh, watch out now! Here comes a wild spray,
Joyful commotion, we're stuck in the fray.

Mixing and swirling, the rivers conspire,
A dance of the droplets we never tire.
Each twist an adventure, each turn makes us cheer,
Let's float on forever, there's nothing to fear!

Interwoven Waters

Together we tumble, in puddles so grand,
Our adventure begins with a slip on the sand.
Ribbons of water twirl, twist, and spin,
Making us giggle, we just can't help within.

Grabbed by the current, we're all in a whirl,
Four friends united, let laughter unfurl.
Battling the waves with our rubber duck foes,
Plopping and bobbing, who knows where it goes?

Raindrops are joining, adding to the mix,
Juggling the splashes, it's our bag of tricks.
Slide down the bank, see the water glide,
Falling together, it's the funnest ride!

In this little world where we splash and we play,
No worries or cares, just a bright sunny day.
With microbes and fish, we caper with glee,
In interwoven waters, forever we'll be!

Echoes of Laughs in the Gentle Breeze

A parrot on a tree sings loud,
Its jokes float off, proud and unbowed.
The squirrels giggle, tails a-twitch,
As the sun sets, no one's a witch.

A turtle wears glasses, quite the sight,
It reads the news, morning to night.
A rabbit hops with jokes to tell,
While foxes chuckle, oh so well.

The wind whispers secrets, soft and sweet,
Of puddles where frogs skip on their feet.
Each rustle in leaves, a punchline new,
In this funny world, there's always a view.

And when the night comes, stars take a stand,
They twinkle like laughter, oh so grand.
A comet zips by, a joke takes flight,
In this lighthearted world, all feels just right.

Sailing Through Waters of Change

A boat that's swaying, oh what a ride,
With ducks as crew, who paddle with pride.
The waves dance and chuckle under the sun,
While fish tell tales of battles won.

Each splash is a giggle, each ripple a grin,
As seagulls honk, 'Hey, let's dive in!'
The captain is clumsy, but no one minds,
He steers with laughter, fate never binds.

A crab in a hat joins in on the fun,
Waving its claws like, 'I'm number one!'
The horizon glows with winks from the stars,
As laughter echoes, dissolving our scars.

In a world that's jolly, rolling and free,
Waves of humor bring joy to the sea.
Floating along, we forget past defeats,
For in every moment, a chuckle repeats.

Tides Brought Together by Fate

Two fish met at dawn, quite by chance,
They twirled in the water, a glimmering dance.
One said, 'You've got fins that are quite divine!'
The other replied, 'And your scales really shine!'

A wise old crab caught their joyful gleam,
He chuckled and said, 'This is quite the dream!
These tides are fickle, but laughs hold us tight,
Float on, my friends, till the fall of night.'

As the sun dips low, a party begins,
With bubbles and giggles, all silly spins.
A clam cracks a joke, pearls take flight,
In this watery world, everything's light.

With each crashing wave, new friendships arise,
Like dolphins and mermaids under bright skies.
Together they glide, through thick and through thin,
In the ebb and the flow, where the fun will begin.

Embracing Eddies of Connection

In a whirlpool of laughs, a snail spins round,
Telling tall tales as it glides back down.
A bubble of joy pops up from the floor,
While a fish in a tux brings snacks to the shore.

A frog playing trumpet adds rhythm to cheer,
Every croak becomes music we can all hear.
The lily pads rock, under moon's glowing face,
In this lively swirl, we all find our place.

With whirlpools of banter, we float and we sway,
Sharing laughter together, come join the display.
As waves break with mirth, we form a grand link,
In the eddies of friendship, we dance and we wink.

So here's to the giggles, the splashes, the fun,
In this world of connection, we shine like the sun.
Each moment a treasure, in bubbles we ride,
Let's paddle through life, and enjoy the tide.

Beneath the Surface of Togetherness

In the water, we all play,
A splash here, a splash there,
Tangled feet, we float astray,
Giggling as we lose our hair.

Rubber ducks go on a quest,
Floating by with silly grace,
Who knew mud would be the best,
In our silly, splashy race?

Rafts collide, oh what a sight,
With laughter echoing so loud,
Just like fish, we take to flight,
A silly, giggly, swimming crowd.

With each tumble, our joy grows,
Beneath the waves, we spin and dive,
Sparkling bubbles, laughter flows,
What a way to feel alive!

Driftwood Dreams and River Echoes

A stick drifts by, a captain's hat,
Oh look, there goes our ride!
But it's just a log, imagine that,
We laugh, and soon we slide.

Our dreams of sailing far and wide,
On rivers made of marshmallow,
But all we really find inside,
Are snacks we munch, and who knows, bro?

With driftwood dreams of pirate gold,
We paddle hard and dance it free,
What treasures do these waters hold?
Just soggy chips, and sticky tea.

Every wave brings silly cheer,
As echoes of our laughter rise,
In playful joy, we hold so dear,
We sail our dreams beneath the skies!

Fluid Bonds of the Heart

We share a laugh, a boat so small,
Bouncing off the waves with glee,
But oh, we're clumsy, what a fall,
Splashing down, just you and me.

With paddles like we're in a race,
Every stroke's a wild ballet,
We might end up in the wrong place,
But we're dancing all the way!

Fluid bonds let laughter flow,
With each splash, our hearts collide,
Even when the winds don't blow,
Together we float, side by side.

As we drift, our worries cease,
In humor, we're forever young,
With love and laughter, we find peace,
In our hearts, we're always sung!

Cascading Emotions Whispered

Oh listen close, the water spills,
Secrets shared with every wave,
From comical jumps to silly thrills,
Whispers soft from what we crave.

We tumble down from slippery rocks,
In fits of laughter, we confess,
Step aside from serious clocks,
Here, nonsense reigns, we must digress!

Cascades of giggles fill the air,
As splashes dance, we spin and roll,
Each drop carries banter, spare,
In this joyful, waterlogged stroll.

With hearts as light as foam on top,
Our bonds are strong, like rippling streams,
In humor's arms, we'll never stop,
For laughter's glow ignites our dreams!

The Gentle Push

In the river, fish do dance,
While ducks all quack, give romance.
A frog leaps high, a splashy show,
But hey! Watch out for that big toe!

Bubbles rise, a giggly cheer,
Water smiles, it's crystal clear.
A turtle grins, slow but spry,
While paddles splash, a splashy pie!

Noodles float, a wiggly race,
As jellybeans make their place.
With every dab, the fun's alive,
In this silly stream, we thrive!

So grab your float and take a ride,
The river's laughter won't subside.
In every wave, a jest will bloom,
Let's paddle on, forget the gloom!

Beneath the Flowing Veil

A playful breeze whispers near,
While otters giggle, full of cheer.
Underneath the rippling sheet,
Fish play hide and seek—what a feat!

A crab with a sideways strut,
Claims it's the star of the cut.
But oops! It trips on a slimy rock,
And belly flops—what a shock!

Rafts made of leaves gently drift,
As nature gives us every gift.
A heron slips, it's quite a sight,
With flapping wings, it takes to flight!

So dive in deep, laugh till you wheeze,
Let's float on joy, take it with ease.
In bubbling streams, there's no regret,
Just silly fun with no offset!

Tide's Whisper

The tide rolls in, a bubbly tease,
As sand crabs scuttle with such ease.
Seagulls squawk, they're quite the clowns,
Stealing fries from unsuspecting towns!

Wave after wave, the giggles grow,
As kids splatter, putting on a show.
A beach ball flies, missed by a shove,
Who knew the ocean had such love?

Buckets fill with treasures galore,
But oh no! Here comes a sea foam store.
Splashing fun as waves collide,
With laughter ringing far and wide.

So ride the surf, embrace the fun,
In this watery world, we all become one.
The laughs are wild, the joys abound,
In the tide's soft laugh, true joy is found!

Confluence of Souls

At the bend where rivers play,
Fishes flaunt in a bright ballet.
A squirrel joins in for the show,
With acorn hats, it steals the glow!

Beavers build a lodge of dreams,
While frogs croak out their funny themes.
They tap dance on the riverbed,
With happy tunes, all fears are shed!

A raccoon stumbles on a log,
Wobbling 'round like an old fog.
The crowd laughs, can't help but cheer,
For nature's jesters, always near!

So join this party, don't be shy,
In confluence, we reach the sky.
With every splash, a smile's born,
In this silly world, we are reborn!

Where Waves Kiss the Shoreline

The sea is a prankster with salty glee,
It tickles my toes, then splashes on me.
Seagulls are laughing, they swoop and they dive,
While I'm dodging water, just trying to thrive.

Each wave brings a story of laughter or woe,
Sandcastles crumble, it's part of the show.
The tide pulls my snack, like a thief in the night,
While crabs scuttle past, it's a comical sight.

I chase after seagulls, they mimic my run,
They squawk at my antics, oh what a fun!
A splash from behind, like a comedian's art,
The ocean's the stage, and I play my part.

So here by the shoreline, I kick at the foam,
With seaweed for hair, I'm quite far from home.
But laughter's the treasure, more than gold in the sand,
In waves full of humor, I take a stand.

Uncharted Depths of Affection

In waters unknown where the fish like to flirt,
I swim with my goggles, but what's that? A shirt?
Lost under the waves, it's a party, I swear,
A fashion show hosted by creatures with flair.

Octopus fashion, with eight arms in style,
Attracts even turtles who dance with a smile.
Each bubble a giggle, a swirl and a twirl,
The seaweed's the confetti, oh what a whirl!

I dive to the depths, but find a lost shoe,
Waves tickle my ribs, oh how do they do?
Fish give me side-eyes, they're judging my spree,
While plankton are snickering, just wait and you'll see.

So here in these waters, the laughter is grand,
With sea creatures prancing, a comedic band.
Uncharted emotions, in waves they do flow,
Life's antics submerged, what a wonderful show.

Surrender to the Flow of Life

Let go of the reins, just drift like a leaf,
While ducks quack in rhythm, oh sweet relief.
The river is giggling, it tickles the shore,
With crayfish debating what life has in store.

I float with the reeds, sharing jokes with the frogs,
While fish flash their smiles and dance in the bogs.
A frog hops beside me, he croaks in delight,
As dragonflies zoom, making life a pure flight.

Oh, bubbles of laughter pop up all around,
As I try to stay steady, but I'm spinning 'round!
The current is quirky, it pulls me with ease,
Like a prankster friend, always ready to tease.

So here on this river, I toss out my fears,
With waves full of humor, I float through the years.
Embrace all the silliness that life offers free,
In laughter, we drift—come and float with me!

Currents Cradled by Moonlight

The moon's got a secret, it winks at the tide,
Whispers of mischief that flow far and wide.
The stars giggle softly, a heavenly crew,
As waves moonwalk by, shimmering in view.

I'm bobbing along with a boogie-board smile,
While jellyfish glow like they're lit with a style.
The current's a dance floor, with splashes of light,
As the crabs do the hustle, what a marvelous sight!

Moonbeams are spinning, a disco so grand,
As fish pull some moves like they've got a band.
I trip on a seaweed, but laugh at the fall,
The ocean's a party, it welcomes us all.

So here in this magic, where laughter does grow,
The tide pulls us in, to a rhythm we know.
With currents of joy wrapped in shimmering night,
We surrender to fun, bathed in silvery light.

The Language of Ripples

In ponds where turtles talk to frogs,
The water giggles, playing tags.
Fish gossip underneath the waves,
While ducks attempt their silly raves.

A splash of joy, a drenching grin,
As crabs do dances from within.
Each ripple sends a secret twirl,
A joke shared 'round by every swirl.

The lilies roll their leafy eyes,
As dragonflies engage in lies.
"I can dive deeper than you see!"
"I can zoom faster!" claims a bee.

So let us laugh at water's art,
As nature teaches us to start.
In whirlpools where hilarity thrives,
We'll find the fun in all our dives.

Whispers in the Flow

The brook prattles like a chattering friend,
Serenading rocks, as bubbles blend.
"Hey, did you hear that fish just tripped?"
"No way! I thought the snail was whipped!"

A leaf swims by, on an awkward ride,
Squirrels cheer from the river side.
"I bet she'll crash!" and splash they do,
A dance of joy, a comical crew.

The waves gossip with ticklish might,
Even shadows are giggling in delight.
As otters juggle their sun-kissed play,
All of nature joins in the fray.

With every swirl, a chuckle grows,
A festivity where laughter flows.
So let the currents keep their jest,
In nature's flow, we find our best.

Undercurrents of Connection

Beneath where bubbles make their sound,
A crab complains, is homeward bound.
"I swear this rock was once my chair,"
"I lost my shoe! The current's unfair!"

The otters twirl in a playful spree,
While minnows buzz with glee, you see.
"You think you're fast? Well, watch me go!"
Said the perch, feeling the river's flow.

But here come the beavers, making a fuss,
"We're building a dam—don't make a fuss!"
And all the fish swim the other way,
As laughter echoes through their play.

With every splash, a friendship's been forged,
In waters where joy's often gorged.
So roll in the eddies, embrace the cheer,
For connection flows as we draw near.

The Embrace of the Depths

In caverns where mischievous shadows creep,
The dolphins tease as their laughter leaps.
"Did you hear about the crab who danced?"
"What a silly move! He's got no chance!"

The starfish plays a game of hide and seek,
While squids share puns that are quite unique.
"I inked my name on a passing boat!"
And laughter bubbles from every note.

Anemones sway with whimsical grace,
Tickled by currents that frolic and race.
"Come join the fun beneath the tides!"
Where giggles and bubbles become our guides.

So plunge into depths of laughter and play,
Let the whimsical waters lead the way.
For in this realm of joy and jest,
The playful depths truly are the best.

Flowing Tides

There once was a fish named Clyde,
Who thought he'd take a joyride.
He jumped and he spun,
In his watery fun,
But forgot about the tide!

He swirled with a wave of glee,
Then got tangled in seaweed free.
With a wink in his eye,
He let out a sigh,
"Just another day for me!"

He twirled with a crab so sly,
Who taught him to dance and fly.
But alas, oh poor Clyde,
Got swept away wide,
His moves were a slapstick high!

Yet every splash was a cheer,
As the ocean rang loud and clear.
So if you see Clyde,
Just know he won't hide,
He's dancing without any fear!

The Song of Serenity

In a pond with a plump little frog,
Who croaked like a blaring old fog.
He crooned every night,
With his utmost delight,
Even scared off a strolling old dog!

His pals all gathered 'round,
For a concert to make the heart pound.
With a splash and a hop,
They danced non-stop,
And forgot the world was quite round!

But one day a bird flew by,
And thought, "I'll give singing a try!"
With a squawk and a cheer,
The frog yelled, "Oh dear!
Stick to flying, oh please, oh my!"

Yet they formed a quirky band,
With rhythms all perfectly planned.
The frog jumped in sync,
And they made quite a clink,
Now they rock all the shores of the land!

Currents of the Heart

A goldfish named Bob had a dream,
To become a star in the stream.
He waved with his fins,
Searched for some sins,
But all he found was some cream!

He practiced his wiggle each day,
Until a puffer fish shouted, "Hey!"
"You swim like a clown,
With a frown upside down,
But I think you're cute anyway!"

So they teamed up and launched their act,
With tricks and great fishy tact.
They flipped and they spun,
Underneath the warm sun,
Who knew that such laughter could attract?

Their bubble show stole the whole scene,
The crowd cheered, feeling quite keen.
With a splash and a swirl,
They made hearts unfurl,
Curtains fell on the happiest screen!

Timeless Waters

In a lake where the ducks go for lunch,
A turtle named Tim had a hunch.
He'd race all the time,
With rhythm and rhyme,
But always got stuck in a crunch!

Through emerald reeds, he would glide,
But swift was the current, his guide.
With a flip and a flop,
He would never stop,
Just to see who was on the outside!

His friends would all joke, full of glee,
"Let's swim with the fish and the bee!"
But poor little Tim,
He just couldn't swim,
So he rolled in a comical spree!

Yet in laughter, they played all day,
In waters where whimsy would sway.
With a cheer and a laugh,
They forgot all the math,
And found joy in each silly display!

Flowing Tides of Connection

In a river of laughs, we float and glide,
With playful splashes, we're on a ride.
Fish tickle our toes, what a silly game,
They wiggle and giggle—we're all the same!

Drifting on donuts, we whirl and spin,
Water fights pretend, let the chaos begin!
Oh look, there's a turtle wearing a hat,
He nods as he knows that we're all a bit fat!

The bubbles we blow float high in the sky,
A fish tries to jump, but then simply sighs.
Together we dance, with our flippers all clumsy,
Life in this stream is perfectly rumbly!

As the sun sets low, our laughter will stay,
Drifting together till the end of the day.
With friends all around, it's a whimsical cheer,
In the joyous tide, there's never a fear!

Whispering Waters of Belonging

Gliding on ripples, we share a wink,
A gaggle of geese join in the sync.
Their honks are like giggles, echoing wide,
In the muddled marsh, we all take pride!

Jumping in lily pads, what a fine chase,
Frogs leaping high, oh, look at that face!
One's in a top hat, another in blue,
Silly old buddies, a well-dressed crew!

Splashing about, we create quite the scene,
Mud on our noses, we reign as the queens!
Nature's a circus, with all of our tricks,
Beneath pouring rain, we laugh as it flicks!

As twilight approaches, we gather and cheer,
Water teeming with joy, celebrate here!
With squishy, wet hugs, we cringe and we beam,
In this silly stream, we live out our dream!

Dance of the Unseen Currents

Waves break with whimsy on a sparkly shore,
We twirl in the tide, longing for more.
Seagulls tag along, with a wink and a squawk,
Their dance is the rhythm, while we just gawk!

Collecting smooth stones, we create a stack,
It tumbles right down, with a funny clack!
Giggles erupt as it falls with a splash,
Who knew such a pile could turn into ash?

Tangled up nets hold fish with flair,
They wiggle and tussle—a slippery pair!
We organize chaos, like a game of charades,
In the dance of confusion, our laughter cascades!

As the sun blazes down, we sigh and we splash,
Chasing the shadows with a glorious dash.
Together we float where the silliness roams,
In this merry dance, we call it our home!

Entwined in Nature's Stream

In the brook's gentle flow, we paddle along,
With sticks for our oars, we sing our own song.
Ducks quack in harmony, joining our jam,
Who needs a choir? We are who we am!

A patch of wild daisies spills on the shore,
We twirl in the petals, then tumble—oh, floor!
Muddy but merry, we rise with a grin,
Who knew nature's blanket could be such a win?

Trees wave their branches, they invite us to play,
We dance 'round their trunks in a wild ballet.
A squirrel gives chase, with a nut in its fist,
In the game of tag, who could ever resist?

As dusk settles down, twinkling lights appear,
Fireflies dance closer, gathering near.
In the twilight's embrace, we whisper and beam,
Entwined in this moment, we share in the dream!

Serenade of the Stream

A fish in a bowler hat, what a sight,
He waltzes with bubbles, oh what delight!
The frogs cheer him on, with a croak and a leap,
As he twirls through the water, they all start to peep.

A turtle in shades joins the bass on a stroll,
Together they giggle, they're taking a roll!
The otters are dancing, they slip and they slide,
While the water bugs laugh as they ride on the tide.

With lilies for trumpets, they play a grand tune,
The moon strokes the surface, it's a party in June!
But watch out for splashes; oh, dodge or you'll fall,
This stream's quite the jokester, it's laughing at all!

So if you venture near, bring your best silly face,
Join the fish in their hats; it's a laugh-filled place!
For nature's a jester, with pranks to display,
In this watery realm, we splash through the day!

Veils of Liquid Light

Beneath the shimmering veil, fish flit and clack,
With a wink and a wiggle, they slide off the track!
A catfish in pearls sings a tune so absurd,
While the minnows all giggle, 'Oh, have you heard?'

The reeds are all swaying, they beckon and tease,
As turtles roll over, they snicker with ease.
A splash from a beaver, with mud on his nose,
He nods to the sunset, in harmony glows.

Frogs wear their crowns, with the best lily bling,
They croak in unison, like they're practicing sing!
The bubbles are rising, a fizzy parade,
In the raucous ballet, no one's left dismayed.

So dive right in, don't forget your silly hat,
Join the parade of silliness, imagine that!
In this bright, bubbling world, joy flows like a stream,
Where laughter is currency, and play is the theme!

Watercolored Emotions

Ducks in a watercolor, bright hues and cheer,
They paddle around, spreading joy far and near!
Their quacks turn to giggles, they sway with a laugh,
As they navigate puddles, on their joyful path.

A snail on a skateboard zooms past in a whirl,
With a shock and a giggle, it gives life a twirl!
The crayfish all chuckle, they're tapping their claws,
As the pollywogs wiggle in their own joyful jaws.

Watercolors bloom by the edge of the shore,
A canvas of laughter, it beckons for more!
Through the splashes and colors, the whimsy ignites,
As the sun paints the river in whimsical lights.

So hold tight to bubble pipes, let's get in the flow,
Let laughter wash over us, let the good times grow!
In this watercolored world, we splash with delight,
Where every drop shimmers and dances in light!

Driftwood Dreams

A stick and a stone, hold a meeting at noon,
They're planning a party, under the pale moon!
While fish don top hats, and turtles wear ties,
The reeds add the music, as the moment flies.

With driftwood as podium, they speak with great flare,
"Who's bringing the snacks? We need snacks over here!"

The laughter is flowing, like waves on the shore,
As dragonflies dart in, and join the uproar.

A friendly old otter cooks up a nice stew,
With cattails and reels, wow, what a view!
While squirrels shoot marshmallows, a sweet buffet treat,
The party extends all the way to the creek.

So when the sun dips low, come join in the dream,
Let the driftwood remind you that life flows like cream!
Together we'll laugh, through the glee and the schemes,
In the whimsical world of our driftwood dreams!

The Language of Rivers

Rivers chat, with giggles and sighs,
They twist and they turn, all wet alibis.
Fish roll their eyes at their gossiping flow,
"Do you hear what they said?!" Oh, how fast they go!

A squirrel dips toes, laughs with delight,
"Hey, look at me, I'm a fish in flight!"
While frogs croak secrets in near-silent glee,
In this wavy world, there's no need to flee.

Beavers debate, their dams a fine art,
"More wood we can use, must follow the chart!"
But balance is key, and they'll soon agree,
It's better to splash and sing joyfully.

A turtle slips by with a wink and a grin,
"Keep up, my friends, let the fun begin!"
As riverbanks laugh with a bubbling cheer,
Nature's own comedy, never severe.

Water's Gentle Hold

Splashing and flapping, the raindrops compete,
They tumble and giggle in innocent feat.
Each droplet a dancer, so light on their toes,
Spinning and swirling, as the sun softly glows.

"Hey, who stole my sunshine?" the puddles all pout,
"I'm a wading pool now, let's jump about!"
Water's embrace wraps all worries away,
Just join in the laughter, come splish-spash and play!

A stream in the park hums a chirpy refrain,
Where ducks wear bow ties in the gentle rain.
They quack little jokes as they paddle around,
While ripples of joy dance, unbound and profound.

So let's wade in laughter, no need for a plan,
With water all around, it's a fun-filled span.
This gentle embrace invites smiles and more,
In the playful delight of an aquatic chore.

Currents of Desire

A playful brook whispers dreams as it flows,
"Catch me if you can!" it chuckles and goes.
While minnows hold races, who'll win? Oh, they'll see,
With giggling giggles, they swim wild and free!

"Hey, Mr. Fish, let's host a grand ball,"
With bubbles for chairs and seaweed for a hall.
Guppies in bow ties, they're dancing in rows,
With splashy confetti that nobody knows.

"Don't slip on those snails!" a wise turtle cries,
While crabs join the sport with their beckoning sighs.
"Oh dear, there's a wave!" Yet still, they all laugh,
Navigating desire on this joyful path.

As the stream evolves with each giggle and twist,
Unfolds the connection not ever to miss.
With each little ripple and dance for the day,
The currents of laughter forever will stay.

Navigating Tranquility

In soapy cascades, where ducks take a dive,
They quack out their stories, so simple, alive.
Each bubble a tale, they're tickled just right,
Floating in laughter, such pure, merry sight.

"Look at me glide!" croaks a frog with a leap,
Spreading joy wide, no secrets to keep.
As breezes declare, "Let's have a good time!"
Nature's a jest, with a splashy rhyme.

Shells hum soft tunes, as they shuffle around,
With a wink and a twirl, they confound and astound.
Let's sail little boats made from leaves and some dreams,
And laugh with the current, until morning beams.

With tranquility dancing on waves of delight,
Water's a laughter, in day and in night.
So come join the revels, let worries take flight,
In this nautical Mirth, everything feels right.

www.ingramcontent.com/pod-product-compliance
Lightning Source LLC
Chambersburg PA
CBHW070310120526
44590CB00017B/2612